continua

continua

Chris Turnbull

CHAUDIERE BOOKS MMXV

for Mark, Struan, Carol and Jamie: paths ~

first: compass

within
each
other
without
ever
petals, touching
amputate grief

shading, as

though repetition

cross. pull
 a (sigh) ~ memory

translate

you can imagine this scene much like a frayed edge. Its interior

resonates personally ~

sharply curved blooms you've disregarded and if could
                                               with a fold
place —   ed metal key
                                               eight to ten
                                               inches

                                               in length

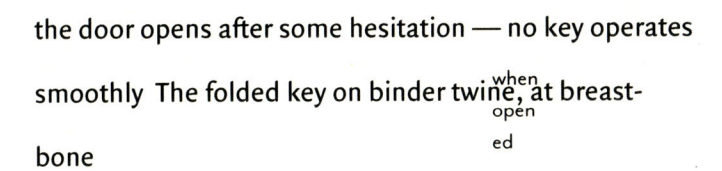

the door opens after some hesitation — no key operates
                                       when
smoothly The folded key on binder twine, at breast-
                                      open
bone   ed

singsingsingsinging
high
notes holding

Your rush is compelled. There are others tucked behind, past,   **sh**   wrecked and
                                                                                         spun
near in, flung, flagging tension. This is how it is done. In the   **uffle up**

background, even breathing has stopped —   the sidewalk

a visceral phenomenon requiring stamina   **with virtue**
                                                                                          sing

                                                                                                an unbound spell

,

Trudy Button says that
              beneath   of leaves
      green is-her-desire is not
the the the the the the the the the
      pa.le infiltration of clouds on eyes

          [f o u n d]

endless

black   those trees at night
              pursue
              white
bugs

essential sensation; beyond being

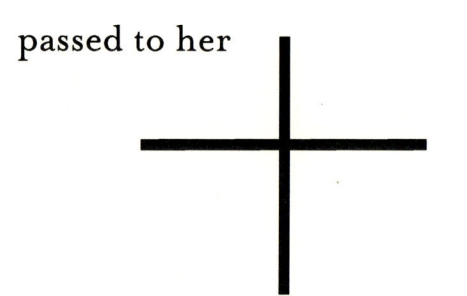

passed to her

                                                             bird bones

stone.stone
someone has gone ahead
stone.stone
someone has gone ahead

next year we'll cut the trees down.
we'll know light again. we'll grow
food in this light. And the forest will
become our window

warble mesic hydric sprawl

milkweed sedum blue (here)
flag iris irus white clover
chicory honeesuckle hawk
weed blackeyed susan wild
basil baysl wild mint ragweed wild
grape bloodroot clintonia yellowlilee
johnny jumpup mayapple red
/white trillium jewelweed (and here)
pond
lily saggilarium star
flower turtlehead & etc/common oth.

[journal disturbance]

          for. each

          flags

          each ditch, each

ea...
gawking &
crowned popular

spadixblaze

, inherited

purple (for) *each of us.*

which we

tell of
very dreams pheromonic
sticky with loci

:snapped branches
:traces on hawthorn pricks
:smoke, wheel ruts
                              tangent to a red
:collections of collections of stones

open: Billy heard pounding pounding pounding
Tunnels are pounding Skin is pounding
             pine heart

cavities vibrant, hollows freed. of. red (cedar)
yellow (birch) red (maple) white (oak). mixed
deciduous

hands inward to chest. ground/canopy . ah — :
close. : Billy hunched nest.

~ burst. a project of territory. spring

       colonies

parsed | rootclutch
alveoli

pain in the belly :

too many crashes :   phantom
                     angelic
                     finite
                     indelible
                     body's
the   disgrace
         ghostly
dives :
, her savvy

[heads. petals ~ looking for systems that will not infiltrate] :
to be lost in a cloud

found

current conditions fair: having fallen will keep falling :

clear the pavement of tourists :

(the canal and its open locks

look look
for   into
   other loss
   ways of
   out place

do.es the act of gravity on the body. do I could

step into the night and be enclosed :with:

for a few infinite seconds, [in it] no conception of top,
bottom or any imaginary centre. That is night hawk.

with time, or then, you may have the beginning of a story:

"if by miracle one means an interruption…"

monarch ~ take

liken

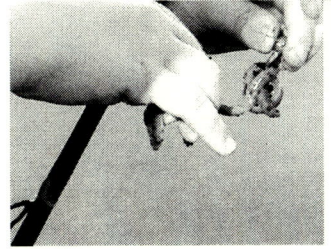

henstone
nestone henstone
lichenstone
limestone plain
limestone pl
lichenstonlichenstone
lichenstone
limestonelimestone p
limestone plai

sticky with loci. shallow with grief

. because
at the mill
the crop
the harvest
are topic —
transaction and plain
conversation no
email
chaff dust and scales
tipped down to future

creek: street

in relief

tempo, rhythm of

horse, the body instrument, the

sublime

axle, even yoke or still paddle

1820: a consistent echo tunnels through the ear canal and winds up the heart.

We weren't so swift or dexterous. We had fixed in our minds that the land would be lush; it would be covered with verdant grass evenly grown and a fine gemmy shade, and sometimes this land would have a tree or so, so captured by the eye in the distance, to rest against for hope and thought, to offer respite and reflection as it were on what we had accomplished and what was yet to be done — as clear as wind's pattern through fields: our final bounty.

We were struck with grief at the immensity of the trees we encountered and their number. They were overpowering in their presence, and we rarely saw the grass that had harboured our dreams unless a pond was present (but it was coarse grass) — yet beside the pond everywhere lay evidence of the ravages of the rodent-scoundrel that gorged itself on the smaller trees and piled its pieces to make its den and produce more of its own kind. It watched us from a sunken state in passages of water or scuttled in the messes along the shore. Bugs crawled in our hair and lit upon our eyes, and mosquitoes attacked our ankles in swarms at dusk or nested in skirt folds.

as when naming becomes her other is sensed as sense and later developed a skin (outer edge)

&

rules to go with it; negotiations

limbs and tendons. It wasn't about worth

It was many near times we would have turned and headed resolute back along the corduroy roads that we'd struggled on to get to this

place.

Our breath was saturated, moist with nostalgia for better times that none as yet felt they'd experienced. The thick canopy overhead, and the midges, had no qualities we recognized, and even our singer was unable to strike a note. We walked the blazes, signs left by the bottle boys, sickened by our own gross mistake and spent by fashionable desire.

you. stand tall off and to the left of an unlit room. stand tall and accented by expectation. stand aware that all ears except yours are attuned to your voice and your throat and what travels there. hunker down and be here. inhabit, anew, this place.

I. suffer from a lack of signification here. I chose this move, am moved. Ah, disruption beyond the physical — a wholly uncomfortable sensation of being that bothers.

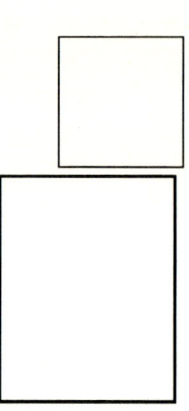

a shine to

                to   always

                    return

              never

  to   always

                      returned

a decommissioned   return
rail line : walking   planned
path bisecting a   never
marsh. Fox,   never
coyote, hare print   returned
the edges   left

        planned

we walk   never
the middle
to no   left
where

[street]: hazardous to cross any particular day because of the angles; the one way sign that doesn't function. The building takes the attention:

it mesmerizes and charms — on a bright sunny day, the sight won't bear it. The front, facing the street, is 3 way glass. The rear, once you're past it, is brick. Your looky-looing has to occur while you're trying to negotiate the traffic, the angles, and the corner. The reflections. No wonder the signs have lost their functions. Nobody can find the hwy.

At night, the appearance of a Japanese silk screen along the entire back inner wall (lit by the headlights of sporadic night traffic) suggests peace and sanctuary. Forget for a moment that the current business is Alarm and Security. The Japanese screen is actually stained glass. Naturally, the building was a general store when the railway industry was central; upstairs was a small school. It's always been occupied by owners interested in parts: alarm and security, engine repair supplies, food supplies; upstairs, always people in transition.

base of a stone wall &
in collapse

Hello, walls.
Driving toward "outside town"
[even though it is not distant
(approx 10 minutes walking
from the former town centre
*marked by a building that
expands a potential point, that
bridges a semi-circle,
like this:

a hard seed

a deep woods song. two o
pposing bridges

configure   a circle

once I told a small tale about a
swooping thing: a bard owl
— still there, a stutter,
a wing in the blood-
stream
go figure

lock. you'd think nothing'd
give way

stone to stone love, plummets here. stone fury, hurl
the stone flat at water surface, a slow melt. ricochet and
indent, line-frets, capillaric: someone will go ahead,
stone, stone dead. to say (i) left that love with

j'oublie

Shudder up to gate bones skin eyes
wrecked by virulence. At the crossing, shake out her umbrella and
wait for passings to turn, her turn. Surroundings straight ocular:
dentist, hitching post, wide-ledge 1/2 house on left. By memory,
water having damaged directions' scrawl. Store with foods of
variety, besides, beside. Closed station across left. Empty space
ragweed and goldenrod and white clover and black eyed Susans
cross right and back one more lot. Danger shack back corner
photographer's ally. Stairs directly across, narrow in breadth, if
not length. Connected here to eatery; wide spaces for sitting on
stop of steps to side. Mosaic, small, on either side of the door,
masoner's doing. Her consideration is stairs here, as much as is
crossing, a looker getting looks oblivious, stride unfeminine yet,
daring to doctor, given to sinners and like women. Bag in hand.

clean window

the eventual deterioration of the street,

oublier

clean me

shudder up to gates shudder bones skin eyes wrecked by virulence. at
the crossing, shake out her umbrella and wait for passings to turn,
her turn. surroundings soft ocular: dentist, hitching post, wide-ledge
1/2 house on left. by memory, water having directed damaged scrawl.
store with foods of variety, besides, beside. closed station across left.
empty space ragweed and goldenrod and clover cross right and back
one more lot deep. danger shack back corner photographer's ally.
stairs directly across, narrow in breadth, if not length. connected here
to eatery; wide spaces for sitting on stop of steps to side. masoner's
doing, small, on either side of the door, mosaics . her consideration
is as much crossing as stairs here, a looker getting looks oblivious,
stride unfeminine yet, daring to doctor, given to sinners and like
women.

got

lost

looking

days clean pass,
I forgets and it
gets away

refusal to permit the closure of form

lichen shows up
stone here,
crenellated musing

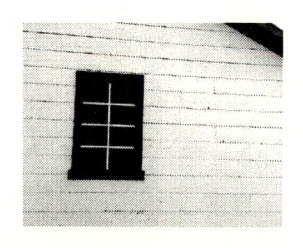

Claire did. Or it was Claire. Without a word	Predictably, the shoe store displayed its new window.	DQ got razed. Walmart got land. Tim Hortons went	Claire should have been a dancer. The overgrown	At the base of a small stone wall
(to us) ditched.	Claire was		acreage stellar	the boys
Maybe we lacked method. She street	glam some other town dancing. She the heart	non-smoking. Our stoop took on the appearance	for woodcocks, and two boys (Billy & Owen)	saw white flecks among wood lilies. Our
as winter and buds spring barely through	of our imagined downtown : a visual pursuit.	of our younger siblings. We phantomed	who often scrammed there on bikes; they were	street dreams a forensic collapse. Lily leaves
the grackles a few days in force.	An unmarked idea taking form.	into minimum wage jobs.	gleaning self-exile from field notes.	split by previous rains

these continua compel
simple facts, some
discomfort. are we no
longer touching now?

memory, too,

holds

this trail hosts compilations of

    the natural:
up past our knees
        signs of enchantment
in ephemeral
        signs of intoxication
pond water. not street
        signs of intercourse
at all
        signs of boredom

        signs of scale

        signs of levity

        signs of ingenuity

            homage

work it.

exclusion. | heartlash.
abandon.
remission.
forgotten.

. letters home

claim, give ~
preoccupied, staked

if she survived the voyage
if her husband or if he survived
the voyage or she
and all found him   take.
by then surviving
a habit : a fortunate
condition for the new
if not a solitary condition for
grief

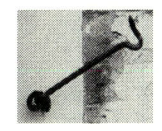

Your language is out down spars
interrupts stalls cloud crowns

words that   , drilled words Words you
describe to replace to   invent
to erode to *desensitized as to live*
                    listening
hold   *forever*

            love,   limber — she
                                       hoists herself
                                       into
   [Claire]

madmen on boats

the city behind

a   seed
vessel

                                              and | then
                                              shh | shh
                                                shh shh

what isn't wounded around here? look at this
hole, the mortar around it, a seed in it some
                           Once, I walked the streets and trails looking for signs
small bird's hope? or wind's chance? or those
                           two bluejays got pissed at me when I crossed into the
three young women lined up on the sidewalk
                           trail — landing in the snow-prints I'd left and pecking at
sketching houses for a school art project —
                           snowfleas, maybe. I felt it may have been more personal.
wearing identical outfits their fashion dictated
                           The season wasn't yet ready for the frogs to unfreeze and
by the only retail store in town, despite the fact
                           the ephemeral ponds to bend and blossom. Some milkweed
that their body shapes are distinctly different. a
                           fluff looked soft against the stiff pods and stems, and in one
cold wind curls down the backside of the boys
                           case I could see where some animal, or some wind, had left a
who wear their jeans low; their shirts ride up. we
                           burr caught up in the silk. If I had gone into the third growth forest,
are strangers to anything but wounds — not far
                           I may have discovered more tracks, at least some chipmunk/squirrel
from here Walmart is moving on; after a decade
                           middens, maybe an old deer chew, but I kept to the trail and ended
of local suspicion that our water is toxic, industry
                           up following the unilingular line of a 26" wheel, which, eventually, got
feels that better profits can be made elsewhere,
                           me lost, and which, in and of itself, signifies zilch.
and so are moving on. demographic is primarily

preteens and aged retirees Council picks are   street is dimdark. whose
                                                             shapes drift at standstill.
slim. we are completed by circumstance.   exquisite : what occurs to interrupt
        it's nice   porchmothbeats::nighthawk: lone kid-throw-rock
                but
        and quiet shh shh   to break
                soon
                                                                            shh shh
            again

second: afterthought: dream
venture

hey there   heyhey there   hey wait,   hey
wait a sec, (let's talk) were we
not in it
   : don't you dare say together we were so :
apart, you keep saying that but don't
you remember
   : no. :
aw, c'mon, you're not still mad
don't be that, c'mon hon
   : don't give me none of your fucking nostalgia, I   lost :
you weren't (heyyy   wait up)
going nowhere, you have to admit it was a good time
(we were) good together
   : aren't you just the lucky one (look at you) :
look, I just came by for old time's
   : sake? look, they took him away right after. I was doped :
oh? so what now
   : I guess I'm never leaving this place :
my parole officer told me I can't leave neither

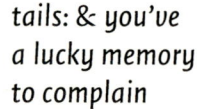

tails: & you've
a lucky memory
to complain

hell, you know
it well, babe

if I hadn't been in
prison we
wouldve gonnon
vacation

letting things take care
of themselves

chronical > polio

the swimming pool a door hidden by grass. record

a natural basin — divert for power, locks, mills

defense: industry : farms

Fast forward when

water sprouted grass, a wading pool

beside it a swing set. The basin to a garden-park.

The custodian < the grass cutter > the raconteur

of locks, water levels, summertime tourists

exclaiming at feats of engineering:

swing bridge, stonework,

crankshaft, the fine toned

arms of the Parks

boys, then

and you see. penultimate freeze-boys hang at the gym-side, hunker with the coach. She

swigs at the moon and highlights verbs such as cackle, boil, cast, hex,

the crickets are autumn as much as their thorax rubs against their

brush of grass against foot tops, metatarsal, and a beat or movement against

it is I who is still

it was Maria: we were all walking to DQ trying to beat
 the heat: a sum
 summer cycle of nothing
 and mosquitoes: nights
 our parents fought in single unit kitchens:
 the housing complex: nous sommes
 we were all born here but
 Maria had been brought in the backseat
 of a 1972 Ford something:
 she was an exotic being
 from nowhere.

right beside

        it [the canal]

        is the yellow plane

   stating
and it hit us as if we'd first woken up.
      the obvious
Claire, who should have been a dancer, twirled
on the sidewalk; the boys
scoping her low slung on wheels,
her humming their humming
spokes and tread

and we all raced to DQ, morphing
town for promise:
a cold
sugar ice
milk / buzz

To the direct left at a 72 degree angle an osprey's concave makings at night a dark, cruddy interstellar kink at the crux of a line. If to take it for motion our transport

history gets to be   stone key archdam
coincidence when   stone key arch
                              damtone key arch
it's lost. let's talk actual right now: dam

progress & building dams. water re-wrote, dissolved,

  Context is forgetting.

           our /
           trace/

cut through bedrock for water
            abandon grief, the hazards
            [for] later generations
exact   will express it with
            buildings believing
we desired

                                                     stone key arch dam
                                                     stone key arch
                                                     dam stone key
                                                     arch dam

street:

calico   lines
the alley [way]
    pools at the knees
          skirts. the broken metal
            escape. stories physical near
    ear suggestion :   needling auditory
blanks

******

even stared
down from the balcony
(hung to brick)
an assembly of users
looking up   star
ing the balcony
down

street:

top cuff button
pushes fashion
glossing
beauty pinks
highs   polish
heels
lush to the
nose lips brow
& disgendered

as if rural

the future mobs the pizza joint. a blitz
of pie shaped paper flutters and flips
shines dimly near gutter. Some poke out of trash cans.

I'd swear angels had exploded mid-air,

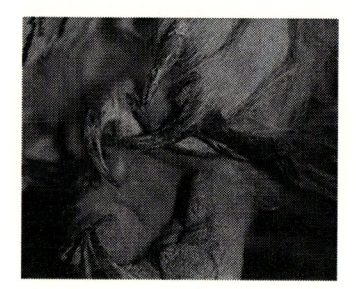

o

in the way some are entranced
by pigeons taking flight, or is it the
spaces they make obvious?

wind

on the highway everything is good. no private distractions like on the street
where you're known

and nothing's new. remember when DQ got razed for Walmart everyone just
figured they'd have more stuff to buy

and we got left

the stoop at first good enough. for pigeons
but where else could we congregate
Joe, Abe, Becky, Gladys — the others

maybe. we'll come back if there's a reunion see how the street

we just have to keep our world outside of here
be tinderbox soldiers

did everyone bring enough
bottled water

flag
iris. rideau

she pops by. a visit after CAS apprehends her kids. tremendously brain-
full, with tumour, (onward). half-seeing she values perception. she
wears a storm on her back. systems fail her. she qualified for low income
retrofitting. she claims her goal is to get an inconsistent answer
from someone. laughs. her fingers grab hold of nothing as she stands
on the porch.

i remember this   she said: Ink blot the psychiatrist asked
what it looked like i said an ink blot & he asked again! I said I get it
it looks like an inkblot. i fell silent — my choice.

that night
hawk

plastic water bottles
Tim Horton's iced
cap(uccino) cups
McDonald's fragments
Tim Horton's coffee
cup lids
Tim Horton's coffee
cups
chip bags
beer bottle necks
to bore/aperture/
throat/orifice
wine bottle pushups
Kokanee and Coors
Light cans
assortment of plastic
bags tightly knotted
containing presumably
dog crap
deconstructed office
chair
beer bottle lids
articles of clothing
separated pairs
Subway sandwich
bags and napkins
condoms
shoelaces
shoe insoles and
tongues

        the state of waste tells the season

        street walk in the woods

        as when the forest

hold on. wait. up
at dog lake's a petro-
glyph a cat from
the boat. the woman re
marked. now there's
two
one's fainter

rock, rock

saddle surface

The hospital marks find that it corners the neighbouring road that takes proper. I think	the town limit; you'd the hwy that leads to town and also the you beyond the town
of healers and who occupy the and towns, thus the inside and the and suspicious.	magicians elsewhere boundaries of villages mediating between outside, both desired A marsh

:small fragments a
flaked rock

centre(less) mediate
friends who disappear
elsewhere   understand
I think their loss   (his)

                & a choice to remove

self &

                not loss (self)

am parallel [even have been (and)

~ a stone weight on distance ~

truant ~
wanderer

echo: I keep my ghosts open

echo: wait

echo: we are meaning

           red-poll
ilence: shatters [when we are not
           eye on window saying]

         all evidence
         of light

         the palm,
         warm,
         a cold-
         gathering
         crescent

yell all

you

want to

you

won't

disturb

the

moths,

feeding

on sap :

as bark

like what? hunched nest? shallow plummet? structural efficiency
has trade-offs. sure I like the forest but transit and currency and urban
mapping ~ scales ~

shhh!

if I asked you would

you disappear (our hover)

with

[finally just you and me
and all this space]

ask you

ask. you

you.

a

grinding
catastrophe

arrive at the same moment. here and overfrom

a crude overhaul.

[plank over water]
[ruff grouse]

where
we are

inside, music attaches. each
note a noise a noise a note

ravenous

(ear parts) 'bell-like' rrrronk

ask.

I

hands specific

whispers for what they are

in our conversation rest

no silence in the flow of breath and arms

                                    not even grace, but I
                                    forget

the session has an end to it

you. I
even separation   even toe-to-toe

mouthmouth over here over from

we

                                         push air fall away

                in

as petals as tongues can be

. so much I

it's unreal

Acknowledgements:

Many have contributed to the shaping of *continua* through conversations, ideas, correspondence, art, photo opportunities, hikes, encouragement, travels, and tangents. You are lovely, and you know who you are. Thank you.

Architect and artist Bàrbara Mesquita provided the apt image for the cover of *continua*. Thank you for your sensitivity to scales, forms, and spaces.

I am very grateful to the editors and publishers who have printed pieces of *continua*, to the hosts of reading venues who have enabled its live performance, to the community of listeners and readers who energize these spaces and after-spaces, and to those who have performed *continua* with me. I am highly appreciative of rob mclennan and Christine McNair of Chaudiere Books. Thank you.

continua was written within a traditional territory of the Anishinaabeg; I offer deep respect to all caretakers of the spaces through which I move and write, and am profoundly thankful for the shared knowledges from which I learn.

A section of *continua* was published as a chapbook : "continua 1-22" (above-ground: 2010). A selection of pieces were published in *Companions & Horizons: An Anthology of Simon Fraser University Poetry*, ed. Stephen Collis (LineBooks: 2005). Excerpts have also appeared online and in print: *Convergences, ditch, Dusie 10, Experimento, Fusebox, How2, Nerve Lantern 8, Ottawater, puddle, Spire,* and *Undercurrents*.

"within each other without ever touching" is from Erwin Hauer's explanation of "Design 3" in *Continua: Architectural Screens and Walls*. "if by miracle one means an interruption" is a fragment of a line in a book by geographer Yi Fu Tuan. Friend and artist Daniel Van Klei provided the image for the page containing "madmen on boats". Bits of the song *It's Oh So Quiet* can be found in "what isn't wounded". It was released in 1951 and sung by Betty Hutton; Bjork covered it in 1995 in her *Post* release.

Elements of *continua* are guided by:

Glenn J. Lockwood: *Smiths Falls: A Social History of the Men and Women in a Rideau Canal Community, 1794-1994* (Smiths Falls: Heritage House Museum. 1994).
Erwin Hauer: *Continua: Architectural Screens and Walls* (Princeton Architectural Press: 2007).
Carol Bennett McCuaig: *Invisible Women* (Juniper Books: 1999).
Any map or mapping tool for the area, either print or online or, in an extended sense, the Rideau Trail map guide, available online or in print form: http://www.rideautrail.org/maps/. Also Heritage House Museum and the Rideau Canal Museum, Smiths Falls, Ontario.

Library and Archives Canada Cataloguing in Publication

Turnbull, Chris, 1972-, author
          continua / Chris Turnbull.

Poems.
ISBN 978-1-928107-04-0 (paperback)

     I. Title.

PS8589.U7428C65 2015   C811'.6   C2015-906149-0

Colophon

Typeset in Adobe InDesign by Chris Turnbull with some corresponding work by Christine McNair. Typefaces used in *continua* are Akagi Pro, Interface Pro, Mr. Eaves Mod, Mrs. Eaves, Quadraat, and Quadraat Sans.

WWW.CHAUDIEREBOOKS.COM